Discovering
EDGED WEAPONS

Major John Wilkinson-Latham

Shire Publications, Tring, Herts.

CONTENTS

1. Early History 3
2. Norman Britain and the Middle Ages 12
3. The sixteenth and seventeenth centuries 19
4. The era of regulation military wearpons 24
5. Presentation swords 30
6. Oriental and native weapons 49
7. Collecting edged weapons 54
8. The identification of edged weapons 58

09/1/2

Published in 2009 by Shire Publications Ltd, Midland House, West Way, Botley, Oxford OX2 0PH, UK.
Copyright © 1972 by John Wilkinson-Latham. First published March, 1972. Reprinted in 2009. Number 124 in the 'Discovering' series. ISBN 978 0 85263 138 6.
All rights reserved. No part of this publication may be reproduced or transmitted in any form or by any means, electronic or mechanical, including photocopy, recording, or any information storage and retrieval system, without permission in writing from the publishers.

Printed in Great Britain by Ashford Colour Press, Unit 600, Fareham Reach, Fareham Road, Gosport, Hampshire PO13 0FW.

Shire Publications is supporting the Woodland Trust, the UK's leading woodland conservation charity, by funding the dedication of trees.

1. EARLY HISTORY

The study of edged weapons is one of absorbing interest and year by year there is a large increase in the number of those whose hobby it has become, combining as it does the fields of history, antiquities and art.

The Stone Age

Prehistoric man's first weapons were without doubt solely for thrusting rather than cutting and consisted of the sharp-pointed branches of trees, either short and of what we can term dagger length, of medium or sword length, or long and of pike or lance length. The need for a cutting edge was obviously apparent but it was not until, possibly entirely by accident, it was realised that the sharp edges of certain stones could slice through skin and bone that early man began to fashion weapons and culinary implements from this material.

Many differing types of stone were used for the manufacture of weapons and of these flint was probably the best, but due to the fact that it occurs only in isolated pockets it was not universally available and basalt, serpentine, obsidian and many others have been found fashioned into knives, hatchets and arrowheads.

Celts. This name for a widely distributed class of weapon has no connection with the Celtic people and is pronounced with a soft C. The most primitive celts found in England are simply flints roughly chipped into shape, and in areas where flint was not a local stone use was made of agate, quartz, granite and even slate. These early celts have been dated to the Palaeolithic period at the beginning of the Stone Age. The next development would appear to be that of grinding an edge by rubbing the roughly chipped stone upon another, possibly with the addition of liberal quantities of water, and many examples can be seen in museums where the result has been a smooth and razor-sharp edge.

The Neolithic period produced many more refinements and celts were polished all over and were in some cases decorated with longitudinal ridges or bored with holes. In use the celt was fixed on to a short haft by either binding it on (fig. 1c) or lashing it into a cleft (fig. 1d) so that it could be used as a chopper in peacetime or as a battleaxe in war.

STONE AGE

Spearheads. The majority of these that are to be seen belong to the Neolithic age and show great care and skill in their preparation, being symmetrical in outline, smoothly finished and in some cases having notches cut in them to facilitate their attachment to the wooden shaft (fig. 2). In size they vary from three to as much as twelve inches long.

Arrowheads. Arrowheads are perhaps the most prolific of all Stone Age finds and range from the early elongated splinters of flint, upon which only sufficient work has been done to effect a sharp point, to the later barbed heads (fig. 1b) which have been carefully shaped and ground to ensure better penetration.

Daggers. Stone daggers and knives have been found in all parts of the world, their prevalence being due to their use as a culinary or agricultural tool as well as a weapon. In the earliest examples (fig. 1a) they consist merely of a crudely fashioned point on an elongated piece of stone, but gradually refinements were introduced and the weapon became leaf-shaped and then notches were made to facilitate the addition of a handle or grip of wood or bone. Grinding produced a keener edge and finally the entire blade was polished.

Battleaxes. Although the celt was employed as a battleaxe a true weapon of this type was made by prehistoric man towards the end of the Stone Age. It had a polished, tapered head and invariably had a hole ground centrally for the insertion of the haft.

As mentioned earlier, the use of stone for tools and weapons was universal but the degree of skill in the fashioning of them differed greatly from country to country. Perhaps the most highly skilled workers were the Egyptians, examples of their work showing beautifully ground edges and much ornamentation. For excellence and elegance of design the Danish hatchets and spearheads were probably unbeatable whilst probably the crudest weapons are the Kelto-Gallic yellow flints found in France.

The Bronze Age

The term 'Bronze Age' is generally used to bridge the gap between the use of stone for weapons and implements and the introduction of iron. There is, however, no doubt that the use of bronze, an alloy of copper and tin, dates back as far as 3000 BC and was contemporary with the latest period

BRONZE AGE CELTS

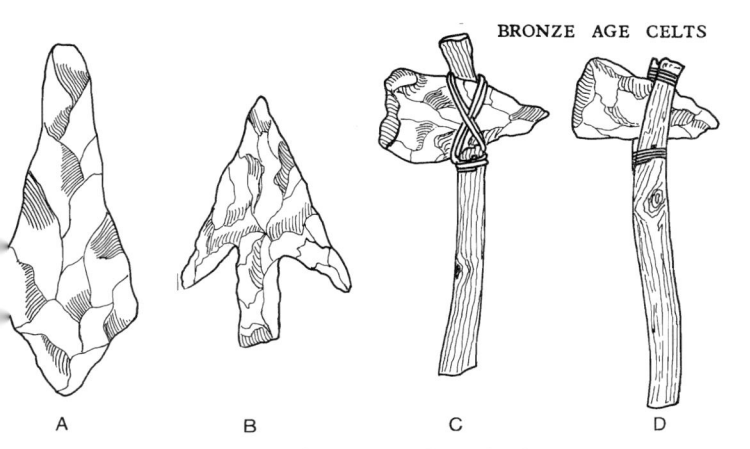

Fig. 1. A. *Early stone dagger;* B. *Barbed flint arrowhead.* C. *and* D. *Early flint axes showing different types of mounting.*

of stone weapons which were superior in holding a cutting edge, and lasted long into the Iron Age because of its relative hardness, which made it preferable to the early iron weapons that bent easily and were then liable to break on being re-straightened.

Celts. These were probably the earliest of the bronze implements and generally followed the same form as their stone predecessors, being used as chisels, wedges for wood splitting, hatchets and battleaxes. They developed rapidly, especially in Egypt, Persia and Assyria and soon took the form of the axe and hatchet that is common today, having a tapering blade and being socketed on to a straight or slightly curved haft.

Daggers. The bronze dagger combined beauty and utility, having a gracefully tapering blade which was usually ribbed down its length to give rigidity whilst saving in weight. In the earlier models, the blade was elongated to form a grip which was later pierced for the attachment of wooden, bone or ivory grips and, as the form of the weapon developed, the

Fig. 2. Flint-headed javelin or lance.

grip became a separate part and was attached to holes bored in the top end of the blade itself. Some daggers were also fitted with pommels which prevented them from being torn from the hand and which acted as a counterbalance to the weight of the blade.

Swords. The bronze sword would appear to have been a development of the early dagger and of all the bronze weapons is perhaps the most graceful. The majority of those that have been discovered are of leaf-shape and double-edged with the tang for the grip being an extension of the blade. It seems that there were two distinct methods of manufacture both of which had their advocates. It was probably in Egypt that the modern method of lost-wax casting was used nearly 4,000 years ago when models were carved in beeswax, covered in clay except for a small hole in the bottom and then placed in the sun which melted the wax out of the mould. Molten bronze was then poured in through the same hole and when it had set hard the clay was broken off to reveal a perfect replica of the original wax model. This method made some of the elegant swords that are to be seen but had the disadvantage of brittleness which could only be partially overcome by reheating or annealing the blade. The second method of manufacture, by hammering or forging the blade from an ingot of bronze, produced a weapon that was workhardened and far more robust than its cast counterpart.

Sword grips were of wood, bone or ivory, riveted to the extension of the blade either as two side pieces or as a hollowed-out cylinder. Although no examples have been found complete with their grips, many have the rivets still in place, either splayed out at the ends by hammering or rounded by the use of a punch. Decoration of the hilt appears to have been fairly common, most being primitively engraved, although some still bear traces of gold which was hammered into an incised pattern.

Although bronze is a metal that is practically impervious to oxidization from the atmosphere, scabbards were used to protect the edges, some sheaths being of copper and others of wood or hide with a copper endpiece.

Spears. Although the spear as a weapon pre-dates even the Stone Age and, as we have seen, spearheads of flint were not uncommon, difficulties of attachment to the shaft prevented the early use of bronze and it is probable that it was not used until man discovered how to cast a hollow socket on to a blade that he was able to secure the shaft satisfactorily.

Some spearheads have been discovered that are tanged and could be bound into a cleft stick, but there are none of undoubted European origin and they could be much later.

There were two basic shapes and of these the sage-leaf design is the more pleasing to the eye, having a central rib that was the extension of the hollow socket and finely ground and polished edges which terminated in a sharp point. The other shape was that of an acute cone, having four or more equally spaced longitudinal ridges, the whole being hollowed to form the socket. The Syrians, Egyptians and Greeks all had bronze spearheads so well designed and fashioned that they are practically indistinguishable from a modern lance-head and the Scandinavian countries produced highly decorated heads, whereas the British and Kelto-Gallic weapons were crude by comparison, although probably equally effective.

Arrowheads. Bronze arrowheads are extremely rare in Britain although they are still to be found in archaeological diggings in Europe and Egypt. Arrows being weapons that by their very nature were continually lost, the use of a rare material like bronze was an uneconomic proposition and it is likely that flint or stone heads were in use throughout the whole of the so-called Bronze Age.

The Greeks

Our knowledge of the Heroic Age of Greece comes almost entirely from Homer whose *Iliad* describes in great detail the weapons and accoutrements of the Grecian soldier. From his descriptions it is certain that the Grecian warrior carried a bronze sword (fig. 3a) with a heavy blade which tapered to an acute point and was decorated with silver studs about the hilt. The scabbard is mentioned, as is the belt from which it was slung around the shoulders, hanging down to the level of the thigh.

The lance or javelin was also a favourite weapon and had a shaft of ash and a head of bronze. It appears that at least six were carried by each soldier and presumably more were available after the first supply had been thrown. It was a deadly weapon in trained hands, in many cases deciding the contest, and it was only on the failure of the javelin that the sword was resorted to.

Arrowheads. The iron arrowhead was the only weapon of that metal in the soldier's equipment, presumably because the working of it was in its infancy and the resulting product was only suitable for a small cutting surface such as the head of an arrow.

The sword. In the Historic Age the sword was of iron but followed the shape and design of the leaf-shaped bronze weapon. Later development, however, gave the Greeks a long, parallel-sided sword with the final point cut to an acute angle and the two edges divided by a strong ridge which gave the blade strength and rigidity. On these weapons and their scabbards they lavished a wealth of decoration and the terminal mount of the scabbard was invariably fashioned in the form of the head of one of the beasts of prey.

The dagger. The dagger was leaf-shaped as was the earlier sword and was known as the *parazonium*. It had a two-edged blade that came to an acute point and the main feature was the amount of decoration that could be put upon such a small object. The spearhead, of iron, was almost the same as the previous bronze model and indeed all spearheads from then onwards look very much alike to all but the expert.

The Romans

The sword. The sword of Imperial Rome (fig. 3b and c) is very similar to that of all the other nations who were in combat with Rome and was of leaf shape but, in comparison with that of her adversaries, comparatively short. In the first century BC it was modified into a weapon of about two feet in length, having a two-edged blade with parallel sides and ending in an obtuse point. The cross-guard was short, the grip was thin and the pommel which completed the weapon was bulbous. This weapon in the hands of the Roman legionary was used successfully against opponents armed with javelin, lance and long sword.

The Roman sword was worn suspended from a shoulder belt and can be seen in considerable detail on the Trajan Column in Rome. Shortly afterwards it was developed into a single-edged weapon known as the *spatha*, which was much longer and was used in the right hand, complemented by the short sword carried in the left hand.

The spear. The *pilum* of the Romans has been romantically called the spear that conquered the world. However, this weapon about which so much has been written is extremely rare and it is doubtful if there were any great number in use. The whole spear and shaft is reputed to have been about seven feet in length, of which the head and socket was one third,

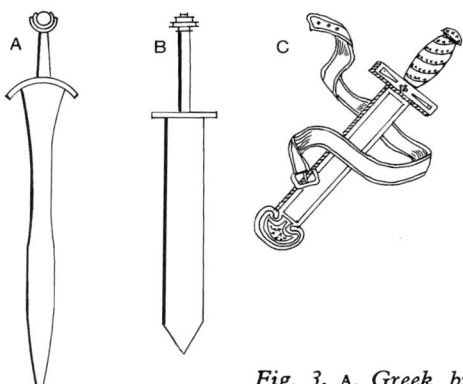

Fig. 3. A. *Greek bronze sword.*
B. *Roman bronze sword.*
C. *Roman iron sword in typical scabbard.*

thus putting the centre of balance well forward and making it into a throwing weapon of great weight. Consequently it is supposed that it was used at short range to blast the shield out of an adversary's grip and make him vulnerable to attack by the short sword.

The dart. This was essentially a Roman weapon and was about three feet in length, feathered at the rear end and tipped with a soft iron point. The main use was against unarmoured troops where penetration of the flesh was likely and its virtue against armoured men was that if it failed to hit a soft part then its point was so bent and twisted that it could not be used against the original thrower.

The Franks

These people, of Germanic origin, having successfully resisted the advance of the Romans in the second and third centuries, commenced their own aggressive migration southwards and eventually subjugated what is now Holland, Belgium, France and parts of Italy and Germany. Their prowess as a military nation was practically without equal and they were formidable opponents. Their weapons were as fearsome as the warriors themselves.

The francisca. This was a missile weapon in the general form of a battleaxe, some being broad of blade and short in the handle and others having a long narrow blade with variously shaped cutting projections on the back end of the blade. This weapon the Franks threw with great force and unerring accuracy for a considerable distance, and the axe was capable of slicing through a leather shield.

The framea or lance. This was the cavalry weapon of the Franks and did not differ much from the lance that was generally in use at the time, the socket being an integral part of the head, held to the shaft by means of one or two rivets.

The angon. This was another missile weapon and was similar to the *pilum* of the Romans. It had a slender barbed head of iron which was from two to three feet in length and was socketed on to a heavy shaft which extended the overall length of the angon to about six feet. It was hurled with great strength and precision and could pierce both the shield and body of an adversary; because of its comparatively heavy weight it could, if lodged in an enemy's shield, drag it from his grasp.

The sword. The Frankish sword was broad, straight in the blade and about 30 inches long. It was parallel- and double-edged, ending in an obtuse point. The cross-guard was a short bar, the pommel small and rounded, and the grip of wood or bone bound with leather thongs. It was carried in a scabbard of wood or iron which was invariably decorated, inlays of copper being usual.

The Saxons and Danes

Saxon and Danish warriors, the forefathers of the present Briton, had as their main weapons spear, sword and axe, and made much use of the bow and arrow.

The spear. The spear was the chief weapon of the Saxon army and was of two distinct patterns. The long spear was a cavalry weapon and the shorter spear was for foot soldiers and could either be used as a defensive weapon or thrown as a javelin. In all Saxon graves, as a rule, a spear is buried with the body and generally speaking the head is of iron and from the remnants of the shaft this seems to have been of ash. This is borne out by illuminated manuscripts which refer to the deceased warrior as the ash-bearer and praise the heroic deeds of the Saxon soldier. From archaeological research it appears certain that the spearhead was of iron and that there were iron cross-guards below the head which were used to ward off sword cuts and other attacks by their adversaries. The cross-guards were not, it appears, an integral part of the head but were inserted into the shaft below the socket. The short spear was usually carried in pairs or threes and the avenging angel, shown in a manuscript in the British Museum, is depicted as having just thrown one, having a second in the right hand poised for throwing and a third gripped in the left hand.

The sword. Among the Anglo-Saxons, the sword was regarded as a cavalry weapon and was not carried by anyone below the rank of thane. The earliest swords that have been found have no cross-guards and merely consist of pommel, grip and blade, which was double-edged and about 30 inches long, terminating in a rounded point. The later Saxon sword was fitted with a cross-piece and the pommel was lobate and ornamented. The grip seems to have been of pine, probably covered in leather. Illuminated manuscripts of the eighth and ninth centuries show swords that are highly decorated with coloured stones and the pommels and cross-guards are shown in yellow which would appear to indicate that they were gold or copper. An example of such a sword in the Wallace Collection in London retains traces of silver work on the quillons. The sheaths for these weapons were probably of wood covered with leather or were made of thick hide upon which ornamental designs were cut, stamped or painted.

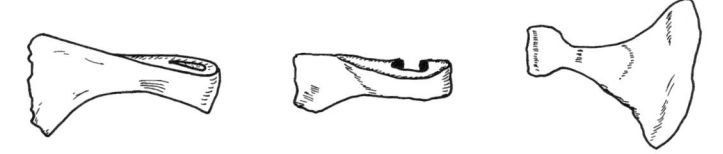

Fig. 4. Saxon and Danish battleaxe heads in bronze.

The axe. Although the Saxons undoubtedly used the axe as a weapon of war few examples exist (fig. 4), but from manuscripts it appears that there were three distinct patterns. The first of these was the broad-axe, which looks very much like a modern tree-felling axe, and the second was the taper-axe which had a longer and narrower blade. The most notable was the third model which was a double-headed weapon either with two blades of identical form or with one blade and a spiked hammer head on the reverse end.

2. NORMAN BRITAIN AND THE MIDDLE AGES

The Norman period

From the date of the Norman conquest of Britain in 1066 our knowledge of the weapons carried in Europe and the Near East is far more accurate. This is mainly due to the profusion of illustrated manuscripts, carvings, monumental effigies and the Bayeux Tapestry. Although there is some doubt of the actual date of the tapestry most authorities agree that it was completed within fifty years of the invasion by William the Conqueror and is, subject to artist's licence, a reliable guide to the arms and armour of the period.

The lance. The Norman lance was very little different from what we have come to expect in the design of this style of weapon. The head was leaf-shaped and, except that it did not have cross-guards, was like the Saxon lance but with the addition of pennons flying from just below the head. These Norman pennons were of coloured cloth decorated to distinguish each body of troops from the others and cut with up to five pointed tails.

The sword. The sword was straight-bladed and double-edged, terminating in a rounded point. The grip, of wood or bone covered with leather, was slightly bulbous and the pommel was usually spherical. The cross-guard was straight at the time of the conquest but by the end of the twelfth century examples can be seen where it curves slightly towards the blade. The scabbards were of wood covered with leather and decorated with stamping or strap work. They were carried suspended from a string or leather thong that was tied about the waist.

The mace. Although not strictly an edged weapon, the mace was used in battle in the same way as the battleaxe but relied on its weight and its blunt head for effect. After seeing the slaughter that was done at the battle of Hastings by Saxon battleaxes, the Normans gradually adopted the weapon in place of the mace.

The Middle Ages

The gisarme. This weapon, known also as the *fauchard,* owes its ancestry to the Bronze Age and is the only weapon that retained its form and style from then until the seventeenth century. It was a double-edged shaft weapon with a blade of up to two feet long, and the back edge was usually fitted with a hook about halfway along its length. As time passed, there were many varieties of blade shape and hook but the general form remained.

The poleaxe. From Saxon times until the end of the fourteenth century the poleaxe was an axe blade on one side of a long shaft complemented by a sharp spike on the other. In the fifteenth century it was developed into a more formidable weapon, the blade being enlarged and the spike becoming a curved pick (fig. 5d and plate 2). It was the favourite weapon of the dismounted soldier after it had been furnished with cross-guards and steel strips along the shaft to prevent the effects of sword and axe blows. Some poleaxes had a pronged hammer head in place of the spike and others had a curved spike on one side balanced by a multi-pronged hammer head on the other.

The halberd. Very like the early poleaxe, the halberd had an axe blade on one side of the shaft and a pointed two-edged blade on the other, but unlike the poleaxe the shaft was continued above the blade in the form of either a sharp spike or a two-edged blade. It was a popular weapon amongst the northern races of Europe and may be seen in many slightly differing forms (fig. 5a and c).

The partisan. Introduced into England and Europe in the middle of the fourteenth century the partisan became a favourite weapon due to the large and fatal wounds that it made. It was especially favoured by the French who used it with great skill and effect. It consists of a long double-edged blade, wide at the base, which is provided with equally shaped projections at the base. These projections were in many different forms from simple spikes to blades of crescent shape. Perhaps the most noted examples today are those carried by the Queen's Bodyguard of the Yeomen of the Guard (fig. 6).

The pike. To the early foot soldier the pike was what the bayonet is today. It was the simplest of weapons being merely a spiked head carried on a straight pole about six feet in length and having the sides of the pole reinforced with steel strips. Some examples of the pike were up to twenty feet in length and were used, with the butt placed firmly in the ground, to receive cavalry. A variation of the pike was the military fork which had a two-pronged head and was sometimes fitted with hooks at the base to remove a mounted man from his horse.

The voulge. This was a variant of the gisarme and in its simplest form was a large blade attached to a short shaft by means of rings (fig. 5e). The blade was normally brought to an acute-angled point. It was mainly a Swiss weapon and found little favour in other parts of Europe.

The bill or war-scythe. In the peasant armies of Europe called at short notice to serve their masters under the system of feudal levy few men possessed weapons of their own and their overlords seldom had enough to arm all their men and so it was that the agricultural scythe remounted on a straight shaft became a weapon of war. At a later date its effectiveness was recognised by its general adoption, and the addition of spikes and hooks to the back of the narrow blade made it a redoubtable weapon (fig. 5f).

The glaive. This weapon differed from the scythe by having the cutting edge on the convex side of the blade rather than upon the concave (fig. 5b). It also had hooks, blades and spurs along the blunter edge and was much used in both France and Germany.

The lance. This weapon of the mounted man did not alter noticeably from its Bronze Age form, although for tournament use the head was blunted and given a multi-ended head of rounded hemispheres. During the period of armoured knights the shaft was fitted with a circular plate to act as a hand guard.

The ranseur. This weapon, a form of partisan, is reputed to have Corsican origins and was called the *corséque* by the French. In shape it was narrow-bladed and acutely pointed, the base being fitted with equi-shaped and pointed barbs which either faced forward, sideways or to the rear. It was much used by French armies and also found favour in Germany and Italy.

The sword. In the Middle Ages the sword of the Norman and pre-Norman periods with the straight double-edged blade, simple cross-guard and pommel was developed much more

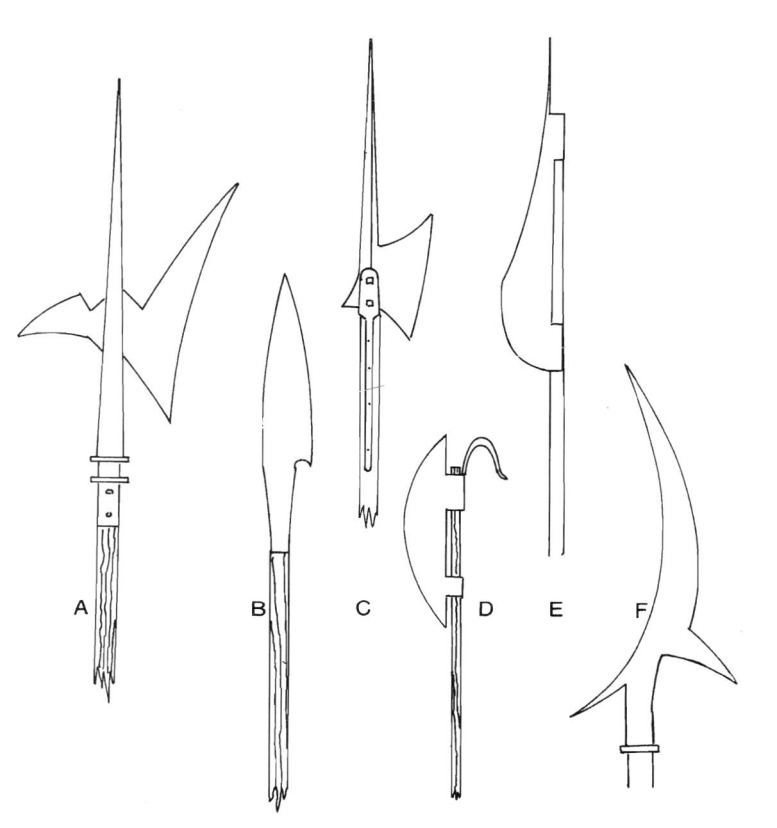

Fig. 5. A. *European halberd, late sixteenth century.* B. *German glaive, sixteenth century.* C. *Swiss halberd, fifteenth century.* D. *Scottish poleaxe, sixteenth century.* E. *Swiss voulge, fourteenth century.* F. *French war scythe, seventeenth century.*

and various forms were in vogue (fig. 7). As the sword progressed the guards became more complex and the pommels were subjected to a higher degree of ornamentation (plates 3 and 4).

The falchion. This was a short sword for archers and had a blade that was curved and widened towards the point. The sharp edge was on the convex side and the back edge was blunt.

Fig. 6. Ceremonial partisans, English, eighteenth century.

The anelace or cinquedea (plate 1). This was a long dagger with a two-edged blade between 18 and 22 inches in length. It owes its alternative name to the form of the blade which was about five fingers wide at the hilt and tapered evenly to an acute point. The crossguard of simple quillons invariably curved towards the blade and the grip was of ivory or ebony slabs fastened to an extension of the blade with decorated rivets. The amount of decoration that was lavished on these weapons was immense and many beautiful examples are to be seen in national collections in Europe.

The scimitar. This, essentially an infantry weapon, was distinguishable by the form of its blade which was between 30 and 35 inches in length, single-edged and widened towards

THE TWO-HANDED SWORD

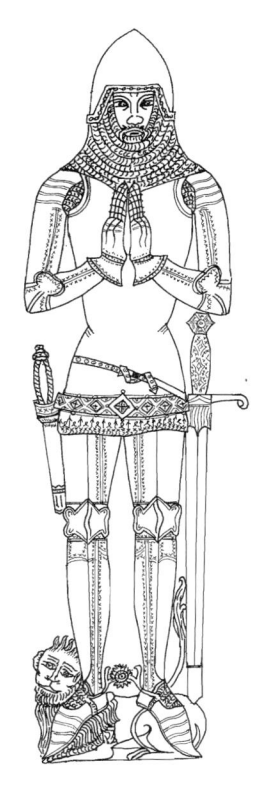

Fig. 7. Thirteenth century knight with sword and dagger, from a contemporary effigy.

the point which differed from the falchion by having a cusp which gave it the shape of a deer's antler. To protect the hand it had a wide cross-guard which was in some cases extended on the sharp side of the blade to envelop the fingers by curving upwards towards the pommel.

The two-handed sword or zweihander. This was an invention of the fourteenth century and was one of the standard weapons of the foot soldier. As its name implies it was gripped in both hands and was used in making wide cutting sweeps which kept the enemy at bay or swept a horseman from his mount before he could come close enough to use his own sword. The Swiss were credited with using it with the pommel bedded in the ground as a defence against charging cavalry, a feat which would seem to demand both great courage and skill.

The sword varied in overall length from about 4 feet 6 inches to over 6 feet, the grip being about 22 inches long and fitted with a heavy pommel to counterbalance the weight of the long blade. The cross-guards normally took the form of wide drooping quillons that terminated in spirals and below them were usually two shorter spiked guards, the origin and use of which appear obscure. In certain examples the blade was wavy and this type has become known as the *flamberge*.

The two-handed sword did not at first find ready acceptance in England although it was much used in Scotland where it took a distinctive form and became known as the *claidheamh-mor* or great-sword. The quillons of the Scottish variety were usually straight although angled towards the blade and terminated in pierced trefoils. The name 'claymore' that has been given to the basket-hilted broadsword of the highlanders is incorrect although it has been universally adopted, even being perpetuated in Dress Regulations for the British Army.

From 1525 to 1600 the two-handed sword was finally adopted in England where it found favour amongst troops who were defending narrow passes and besieged towns where a few men could block a confined space.

The hand-and-a-half sword or bastard sword. This was a large weapon that could be wielded with one hand but was more effective when the pommel was gripped in the other hand to act as a steadier. It had its origin in Germany but soon was adopted throughout Europe and had a vogue in England as the saddle-sword of mounted knights who used it when their lance was broken or they were dismounted. It was in use throughout the whole of the fifteenth century.

The dagger. This diminutive of the sword came into prominence in the Middle Ages in the forms of the *misericorde* or stiletto, used to give the *coup-de-grace* to an unhorsed armoured adversary, and the *panzerbrecher* which was the German equivalent. The *baselard* was a small stiletto which was carried by ladies attached to their girdles as a means of self-defence, although history relates the many occasions when it was employed in a most offensive manner.

The *main-gauche* was a dagger of continental origin which achieved great popularity throughout Europe amongst those who fought individual combats with the lighter type of swords that became familiar in the fifteenth century. This dagger was usually a smaller copy of the actual sword and, as its name implies, was carried in the left hand and was used for parrying and guarding until the time came for its offensive use for the final blows of the fight.

The sword-breaker was a German version of the main-gauche and was equipped with a serrated edge of castellated form which was used to catch the blade of an opponent's weapon and snap off the point.

The Highland *dirk* (plate 11) with its long triangular blade, was used as both an offensive and a defensive weapon and was carried by nearly all Scottish warriors. When the broadsword was used the dirk became a type of main-gauche, but otherwise it was employed solely as a stabbing and cutting weapon and for culinary use.

3. THE SIXTEENTH AND SEVENTEENTH CENTURIES

For two hundred or so years following the end of the fifteenth century, although pole-arms changed very little in form and gradually became less favoured as weapons of war due to the more general introduction of the firearm, the sword became more popular and was developed greatly. This post-medieval period saw the gradual decline of the tournament or 'lists' and the upsurge of the duel as a means of settling individual differences and with this change the adoption of the sword as an item of everyday wear by gentlemen. The use of armour was in decline and some protection for the hand was needed in place of the metal gauntlet that had previously been worn: the answer was the basket, half-basket and cup guards upon which such care and expense was to be lavished.

There was no sudden change and the zweihander and bastard swords continued to be used at least until the end of the sixteenth century, and the ordinary foot soldier still had recourse to his falchion or scimitar when his arquebus ran out of powder or shot, but the gradual adoption of lighter thrusting swords revolutionized the art of swordsmanship and brought with it the early schools of fence.

The rapier. There is no doubt that the rapier was of continental origin but whether its forebears were from Italy or Spain is still one of the many historical mysteries. True, the name could have come from *espada ropera*, which means costume sword in Spanish, but it could also come equally well from the French *raspière* or the Spanish *raspar*, whilst some believe that it stems from the German *rappen* or *raffen*, to tear out.

The rapier in its many forms persisted throughout the sixteenth and seventeenth centuries as a thin-bladed thrusting weapon with a cross-section that was either square, diamond-shaped or triangular and, regardless of the hilt form, only the slim and obviously thrusting swords are rapiers whilst the others are categorised as estocs, sabres, backswords or just swords.

The guard form of the sixteenth century rapier was known as the swept hilt and consisted, in addition to its long cross-guard, of many counter-guards and a knucklebow (fig. 8). The intricacies of the many styles of swept hilt are immense and the decoration of the pommels and the bars that formed the protective parts of the guard are the signature of the craftsmen who fabricated them. The blades are mostly Spanish from the noted factories of Toledo where it was supposed there were special properties in the waters that were used to cure or temper the steel, but it is more likely that at that time the Spanish ores produced a better grade of steel than was available elsewhere.

The cup-hilt was a product of Spain in the seventeenth century and at first was a simple pierced bowl without any sort of knuckle guard other than a simple bar cross-guard, which meant that there was no preferred way in which the sword should be held. Lack of protection, however, soon persuaded the swordsmiths to add a knucklebow and the later examples of the cup-hilted rapier are splendid indeed, with their filigreed bowls, chased quillons and knucklebows and their exquisitely worked pommels.

The dusack. This was a Bohemian sabre of peculiar form in that it had no distinct hilt but the blade was terminated in a ring which fitted the hand and formed the grip and guard. In most cases it was used with a gauntlet to protect the exposed hand and was reputed to be the favoured weapon of the Mussulmans, each of whose swords bore a special name. Mohammed, the founder of Islam, was credited with the possession of nine of these swords, the most famous of which were named Mabur, Al-Adhb, Daulfakar and Al-Kadib.

The braquemart or malchus. This was an Italian sword which was akin to the cinquedea but was longer in the blade. The cross-guard was usually straight and the blade was indented throughout its length with a fuller or indented gutter which gave it strength and rigidity.

BROADSWORD

The schiavona. This basket-hilted sword was the offensive weapon of the Schiavoni, who were the guards of the Doge of Venice. Many authorities claim that the Scottish broadsword and the weapons of the Cromwellian cavalry were descended from the schiavona, but it seems likely that the same form of guard was developed both in Britain and Italy at about the same time.

The basket-hilted broadsword. Known erroneously as the 'claymore', this was the traditional sword of the highlanders of Scotland and can usually be identified by its double-edged blade which bears one or two fullers along its length. As a cavalry weapon it is called a 'backsword' and is then single-edged and has a broad, strong back on the blade to add weight and strength. Some of the basket hilts of horsemen's swords have a large cut-out on the left-hand side of the guard through which the reins could be passed so that the sword hand could be used to control the mount at the same time as the sword was held at the ready.

The small-sword. This exquisite little weapon has for a long time fascinated collectors of edged weapons throughout the world. Once the sword became a weapon that was carried by the gentleman in everyday civilian attire, as the umbrella is today, common sense prevailed against the need to carry

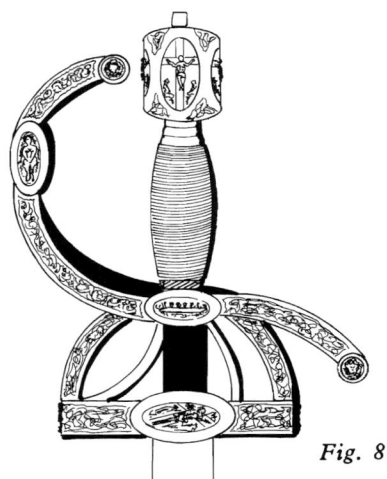

Fig. 8. The sword of Spinola, Brescian, 1600.

anything but the lightest of swords and with the formation of the Standing Army in 1660 the carrying of heavy weapons could be left to the professional soldier. Thus was born the sword that has been known as the 'walking', 'town', 'court' or 'small' sword.

The blade of this weapon was always straight and about 32 inches in length and generally speaking the earliest examples had modified rapier blades of double-convex, diamond or hexagonal section. Very soon, however, the triangular-section blade was introduced having a broad base on the inside and two shorter equal sides. A later development produced the *colichemarde* blade which was a broad-based triangle for the top 6 to 8 inches near the hilt and then tapered abruptly to an isosceles triangle for the remainder of its length.

The treasure that lies in the small sword is in the hilt, which became the product of the goldsmith, silversmith and jeweller, rather than of the cutler and hiltmaker (plate 7). These hilts ranged from simple steel to the most elaborate creations of gold, silver and jewels. Fabergé, who was court jeweller to the tsars of Russia, produced hilts that are treasured today as some of the most beautiful that were created. The basic parts of a small-sword hilt were the pommel, which was usually of hollowed-out filigree work, the knuckle-guard and shell which were either of silver or silver decorated with gold inlay, and the grip which was either a wooden former bound with silver or gold wire, or was made of precious metal and inlaid with jewels.

The pillow sword. This name is the invention of some romantic historian and not the correct nomenclature for a particular type of sword. The weapon referred to is a small variety of the town sword and it was supposed that it was hung beside the bed, probably from the supports of the four-poster in case of attack by intruders. There is no evidence to support this view and in fact the sword is a diminutive of the small-sword mentioned above. They differ only in the lack of a knuckle-bow and the simplicity of their decoration.

The mortuary sword. Once again this name seems to be an invention of the modern collector of weapons and is given to swords that bear on their cross-guards a head of King Charles I. There would appear to be no evidence to suggest that these swords were anything but decorative and in fact some antedate the king's death by many years.

Calendar swords. These are not in themselves a specific style of weapon but are solely swords that bear, by way of decoration, a perpetual calendar embossed along the length of the blade.

Staff weapons

As mentioned above, pole weapons changed little in character during the sixteenth and seventeenth centuries. There were, however, two additions to the range that were important and a variation of an older weapon that caught the imagination of both soldiers and public alike.

The linstock. This was not originally designed as a weapon but solely as a pole on which to carry a long-burning match for igniting early cannon. It had a branched head like the military fork, and at the end of each branch was a clip for the match, but in some cases a blade was introduced between the branches to make it into a weapon.

The spontoon. This was a pole weapon that replaced the pike for infantry and had a leaf-shaped blade and a short cross-bar, for defensive purposes. Its name derives from the French *esponton,* a type of dagger, and it became the badge of command in the British army, being carried by both officers and sergeants as late as the middle of the nineteenth century.

The tomahawk. This was a derivative of the North American Indian's axe which was used by him both as an agricultural implement and as a weapon. Originally a stone-headed axe, it was copied in both steel and brass by the earlier settlers of America and found its way on to the European market through the return of travellers and the acceptance by British troops of its effectiveness as a weapon.

In form the tomahawk is like a normal hatchet with the weight of the cutting head balanced by a short spike on the reverse or a tobacco pipe that is smoked through a hole pierced along the length of the shaft.

The bow and arrow. Despite the rise in the use of firearms, the bow and arrow and their successor, the crossbow, continued to have an important place in small wars. In clan warfare in Scotland the 'cloth-yard', as the arrow became known, had an important bearing on the result of battles and the steel tip of the arrow, forged by hand from the off-cuts of sword blades, allowed a well-shot arrow to pierce the bodies of two men standing in line.

The crossbow fired a bolt, rather than an arrow, and this was usually forged from one piece of steel, the offensive end being simply a point, although in some cases a broadened cutting edge was added.

4. THE ERA OF REGULATION MILITARY WEAPONS

The eighteenth century heralded the beginning of the equipment of armies to regulation and the documentation of the various patterns of weapons, uniforms and accoutrements. It is probable that the first orders regarding edged weapons came at least a century before, but they were couched in such general terms that they could not be regarded as firm regulations of the exact type or pattern that was to be carried by the various branches of the services.

The forerunners of the regulation armies were without doubt those of Prussia and France and by about 1705 the forces of other European countries had followed suit. Early regulations were not, however, in the descriptive form that we know today and the majority of them were devoid of any sort of drawing. Consequently commanding officers and manufacturers interpreted them in widely differing ways so that the end products were almost as diverse as they had been before the approved patterns were prescribed.

In 1822, two years after the accession of George IV, many new regulations were promulgated and on this occasion the descriptions were written in a far less ambiguous way. Actual patterns of the weapons were lodged at the Tower of London and each one was sealed with the mark of the Board of Ordnance. These 'sealed' patterns were made available to manufacturers who could then see the exact style of the hilt, blade and scabbard of swords and bayonets and the exact details of polearms. At least since the early days of this century the 'pattern' room has been at the Royal Small Arms Factory at Enfield Lock and it contains patterns of most of the personal weapons of the British soldier for the last hundred years. It may be visited by appointment.

The study of 'regulation' edged weapons is complicated by the large variety of patterns within the individual armies and by the similarities that exist between styles adopted by various European and American governments. Most armies had slightly differing patterns for officers and other ranks and special weapons for pioneers, musicians, officer-cadets, engineers and their quasi-military forces such as the police and in Germany even firemen.

Military swords

With swords it is possible to generalise to a certain extent by dividing the weapons into two groups; those used by mounted troops and those used by foot troops. The predominant users of the sword were the cavalry and generally they carried a comparatively heavy weapon with a straight or slightly curved blade that was designed with the cut as its primary function. The hilt was usually a basket or shell that gave protection to the hand and was of sufficient size to accommodate it comfortably when a thick glove or gauntlet

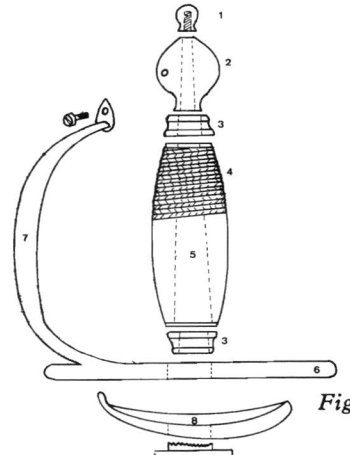

Fig. 9. The parts of the regulation military sword: 1. top nut, 2. pommel, 3. ferrule, 4. grip, 5. tang of blade, 6. quillons, 7. knuckle-bow, 8. shell guard.

was worn. Foot troops, when equipped with the sword, normally carried a straight-bladed and much lighter weapon which was developed from the town or walking sword of the seventeenth and eighteenth centuries, with its simple knuckle-bow hilt. If of junior rank the foot soldier was usually equipped with a short curved sword of the falchion type which was known as a hanger.

In the seventeenth century wars against the Turks, the Polish and Hungarian armies employed what they termed light cavalry and the success that was achieved by these well-mounted, lightly armed troops was such that other

SABRES AND BROADSWORDS

European armies soon followed suit and divided their mounted forces into heavy and light regiments. The weapon of the light cavalry was the sabre, a broad-bladed single-edged sword with a curved cutting edge and a simple hilt consisting of a pommel, grip and cross-guard. However, it was soon apparent that the guard gave little or no protection to the hand and so the front side of it was then extended, bent around the knuckle and joined to the pommel, forming what became known as the stirrup hilt from its resemblance to half a stirrup iron. There is a legend that a certain regiment of light dragoons, being dissatisfied with their simple cross hilt, replaced the regulation guards with locally manufactured knuckle-bows made from discarded stirrup irons but none of the regimental historians lays claim to this fact and it would seem to be a figment of someone's imagination.

Warfare was rapidly becoming a science and the widely differing terrains that were being fought over in America, India and the Far East became the spawning grounds for new ideas and techniques. The creation of specialised bodies of troops such as grenadier companies, who were expert in arming and throwing grenades, light companies, whose speciality was skirmishing in front of the advancing infantry in situations which were not suitable for the use of cavalry, and the various types of combat engineers produced requirements for lighter and more easily manageable weapons than were prescribed by regulations and led to the adoption, and finally the official approval, of different patterns of swords and bayonets.

The basket hilt, familiar today on the Scottish broadsword, was used by the German Landsknecht troops as early as the sixteenth century and was adopted by the mounted regiments of Cromwellians and Royalists in the seventeenth century. However, by the beginning of the nineteenth century it had become solely the ceremonial hilt of Highland swords, its decease being due to the unwieldiness of a sword equipped with it and the cramping effect it had upon the hand if used for long periods, and in its place the simple bowl or knuckle-bow was used. On Highland broadswords the basket was removed for active service and replaced by a simple cross-guard of regimental design.

Infantry swords and later cavalry weapons had, in place of a basket, either a steel bowl guard or a half-basket, made either from separate bars or of pierced sheet metal, and the best examples are the three-bar light cavalry hilt of 1822 (plate 8) which is still in current use for the Royal Artillery and the Royal Corps of Transport and the 'gothic' hilt of the 1822

NEW PATTERN SWORDS

infantry sword which was carried until 1892 by many branches of the British Army and is still carried by the Brigade of Guards, the Rifle Regiments and the army of the Republic of Ireland.

After the Crimean War and the Indian Mutiny the sword ceased to be a primary weapon for infantry officers, for whom the revolver had been ordered, and had been superseded for lower ranks who had previously carried it by the issue of rifles and bayonets.

For cavalry the sword was still the fighting weapon and was carried in conjunction with the lance or carbine, neither of which was effective at close quarters. In 1853, for the first time for many hundreds of years, the distinction, as far as swords were concerned, between heavy and light cavalry came to an end with the issue to all troopers of the pattern sword of that year which was of a new design; it had a curved single-edged blade which continued up through the guard to form the basis of the handle on to which two side plates of leather were riveted. The guard was of three steel bars like the officer's sword of 1822 and whilst it gave good protection against an enemy sword cut it was particularly vulnerable to a thrust from sword or lance.

In 1864 a new sword was prescribed for cavalry troopers that had a very similar blade to the pattern of 1853 but had a guard which was made from sheet steel with, for decorative purposes, a small pierced pattern of a Maltese cross on the front. This gave added protection from both the cut and the thrust but regrettably the quality of the blades was extremely poor and the weapon behaved so badly in battle that reports on it soon reached the British public at home, resulting in a huge arms scandal. To the failure of the swords there were soon added further reports of bayonets that bent and curled up like corkscrews and rifles and cartridges that jammed or failed to fire.

Immediate steps were taken to remedy the complaints about swords but the root cause of the trouble, which was the incorrect hardening and tempering of the blades, was not attended to and the next new weapon, issued in 1882, incorporating the same guard with a modified blade, was no better than its predecessor. As a result a War Office committee was formed to discuss and recommend any changes that were required but sad to say its deliberations did not produce anything that was at all novel and the pattern swords of 1890 and 1899 were almost as faulty as those that had gone before. The committee was thereupon reconstituted and ordered to study the swords of other European nations together with all the evidence that was available from cavalry regiments and as a result it ordered in 1904 a completely new style of weapon that was issued to certain regiments for trial.

The trials were eminently successful and with slight modifications the sword became the trooper's pattern of 1908, having a long and strong single-edged blade of almost rapier thinness and a large bowled guard with a grip that was specifically designed to fit the hand and to bring the weapon to the point position without effort.

The mameluke sword

Another style of sword that had great popularity amongst cavalry officers owed its origin to the tribesmen of India, where much nineteenth century soldiering was done. This was the mameluke pattern of sword which had a blade of razor sharpness and was curved to a varying degree, depending upon the whim of the user, some weapons being so extravagantly curved that they would have been almost useless for fighting. This was solely and simply a ceremonial sword and was carried at levees and in full dress, the cross-guard being very simple and of regimental design and the grip of ivory, either plain, chequered or carved. The scabbards in which these blades were sheathed were also of regimental design and varied from the simple black leather with gilt mounts to the extravagant use of shagreen for a covering and silver-gilt filigree mounts that extended for the entire length of the scabbard.

A simple version of the mameluke sword had been presented to the Duke of Wellington after his successful campaign in India and when he became commander-in-chief of the army he ordered that all field-marshals and generals should carry such a weapon and today, 140 years later, these officers carry the same pattern, making it perhaps the longest-lived weapon in use in the British Army.

The lance

Mention has been made of the lance that was carried by cavalry troopers. The lance had gone out of vogue in the seventeenth century and was only re-adopted after the success of the Polish lancers in the service of Napoleon. In the British army the first of the new lances was taken into service in 1816 and was a copy of one of the French lances that had been brought to this country as a souvenir. Its 16-foot length was soon found to be unwieldy and a Horse Guards committee recommended the adoption of one of only 9 feet in length and this, with a variety of head designs, has been adhered to since then.

The Boer War saw the end of the lance as a practical weapon of war and although there are records of its use as late as 1917 in Palestine it was obviously no match for the concentrated fire of rifles and machine-guns which cut down the horses and men long before they could get within effective distance. It can still be seen today in the ceremonial ride of the Household Cavalry at the Royal Windsor Horse Show, but nineteenth century pageantry and twentieth century warfare are now poles apart.

The bayonet

Between the adoption of the Brown Bess musket in 1730 and the modern self-loading rifle there have been well over a hundred different patterns of regulation bayonet in the British army. The origin of the bayonet and its name are a matter of conjecture but it seems evident that it was either a dagger or a broken arrow (the old French word for arrow is *bayon*) that was put into the discharged barrel of an arquebus or musket so that it could be used as a pike.

The first bayonets were known as plug bayonets (plate 9) because they had handles that could be forced into the barrel in the manner of a plug. These, however, led to damaged barrels and some could not be readily unplugged, so a new design was introduced with rings that fitted around the outside of the bore and thus allowed the piece to be fired with the bayonet in place. Theory, however, did not go hand in hand with practice and the bayonets seldom stayed in position on the musket until the adoption of the French method of a split socket that could be squeezed into the correct size for any particular barrel.

The socket bayonet (plate 10) and variations of it remained in British service for about 150 years and for the majority of this time the blade was to be of triangular section. In 1800 the Baker rifle was selected at the firearms trials at Woolwich for use by light infantry and with it Ezekiel Baker supplied a flat-bladed sword bayonet some 27 inches in overall length and, with variations, this remained in service until the first of the percussion rifles, the Brunswick, was ordered in 1836, also for light infantry. Meanwhile the infantry were still equipped with the Brown Bess and spike bayonet. The Brunswick also had a sword bayonet that was very like the early patterns of Baker.

The Minié Enfield and Snider rifles all utilised the socket triangular bayonet and it was the socket bayonet on the Martini-Henry rifle of 1876 that was responsible for the bayonet's share of the great arms scandals of the latter part of the nineteenth century. In 1888 the sword bayonet superseded the triangular type and from then until the re-adoption of socket spike bayonets on the Number 4 rifle of the Second World War all British rifles were equipped with sword bayonets.

Trench weapons

Axes and billhooks had no part to play as weapons in the era of regulation weapons but were much used as pioneer, engineer and infantry tools, and only in extreme cases such as occurred during trench raids in the First World War were they pressed into use in attack or defence.

Knives had a great vogue as trench fighting weapons during the First World War but none of them was regulation and it was not until the formation of the Commandos in 1940 that an official fighting knife was ordered. This was the Fairburn and Sykes knife that was designed by two ex-officers of the Shanghai police in conjunction with the Wilkinson Sword Company, and over a quarter of a million of these were made and issued.

5. PRESENTATION SWORDS

The sword has always been a symbol of manhood, the young gentleman of medieval days receiving his first sword as a gift from his father when he was considered to be of sufficient maturity. In the days of the Crusades it also became an emblem of Christianity, each knight using his cross-hilted sword fixed blade downwards in the ground as his personal altar for his morning devotions.

The presentation of a sword has, since time immemorial, always been the accepted method of rewarding a warrior for his success in battle or indicating to a king the respect that his friends or even enemies have for the warlike conduct of his people. Although of late the fashion of presenting martial tokens has become rare the successful generals and admirals of the First World War were each given a sword by the City of London at the time of the granting of their freedom of the City and perhaps the best-known presentation was that of the Sword of Stalingrad, now preserved in the rebuilt museums in that city (Volgograd today), which was the gift of King George VI to the people of Stalingrad as a token of the esteem of the British people for their heroic defence of their city.

TRAFALGAR SWORDS

In 1803 there was formed in London the Patriotic Fund of Lloyd's with the specific intention of rewarding distinguished feats in naval warfare by the presentation of a suitably inscribed sword and sword-belt. The style of sword having been agreed upon it was decided that there would be three classes of weapon, the highest class being a sword of the value of £100 intended for captains and commanders. The second class was a £50 sword for lieutenants and the lowest class a £30 weapon for midshipmen, masters and mates. In addition there was a special Trafalgar sword which was a variation on the £100 class.

There are differing estimates of the number of swords that were actually presented, one authority putting the total of £100 and Trafalgar swords at 68 and the total of £50 swords being variously 28 or 82, depending on which authority is quoted, but all seem to agree that the £30 weapon was the smallest total at 16. In the end, the presentation was not restricted to the grades of officer or warrant officer that were originally prescribed, two of the £100 swords going to lieutenants and two to army officers, nine of the £50 swords going to Royal Marine officers and fifteen to captains in the naval service of the Honourable East India Company. The fund only operated for seven years and ceased to operate in 1809 by which time they had made presentations of plate and swords to the value of £21,274.

The Lloyd's swords were all supplied by Richard Teed, who had set up business in the Strand as a jeweller and dealer in antiquities in 1797. From 1806 onwards he described himself on his trade cards as 'Dress sword maker to the Patriotic Fund' but there is little doubt that he only made the hilts and scabbard mounts, buying the blades in from established sword makers, the name of Runkell of Solingen having many advocates.

The Honourable East India Company also gave a large number of presentation weapons to its many officers both for deeds of war and for services to the company in its task of administering the people of the countries which it controlled. A notable example of an H.E.I.C. sword is that of Lieutenant Samuel Snooks, now in the National Army Museum, which was official recognition for the manner in which he looked after a number of native islanders who were stranded in India and at his own expense fed and clothed them and then chartered a small ship to return them to their island.

For special gifts from or to royalty the bejewelled sword was fashionable and could be as plain or elaborate as the depth of the donor's pocket indicated. King George III presented Admiral Lord Howe, in recognition of his leadership of the fleet on the 'Glorious First of June' in 1794, with a diamond-hilted small sword which was valued at that time at £3,000 and in 1910 the Maharaja of Jeypore's coronation gift to King George V was a mameluke-hilted scimitar with the hilt and scabbard encrusted with diamonds to the value of £10,000 which today must be worth at least five times as much.

On the lower scale, the fashion of officers clubbing together to present one of their number with a sword on his promotion or succession to command was much in evidence in the volunteer forces in the nineteenth century and many of these, mainly regulation weapons, are in antique shops and salerooms today and in fact some collectors specialise in the acquisition of these. Lately, unfortunately there has been a certain amount of minor forgery in the antique weapon business and some weapons now bear inscriptions that they did not originally have and which have been added simply to enhance the value of the weapon. Generally speaking an original inscription can be identified by the style of the embossing and lettering which should all be cut to the same depth in the metal but deep polishing can reduce all the markings to the same level and then only an expert can tell the genuineness of the piece.

Simple presentations to comparatively unknown personages are hardly worth forging and are therefore probably genuine but those given by or to royalty and those that are presented to famous military and naval officers should be accompanied by documentary evidence if and when they are purchased. An example of an authentic inscription of the Victorian era would probably be of the following type:

PRESENTED TO LT. COL. SIR ARTHUR KNEEBLAST, KCVO, BY THE MAYOR, ALDERMEN AND COUNCILLORS OF WIDNES UPON HIS RETURN FROM THE CRIMEAN WAR. MARCH, 1855

An example of an obvious forgery that the author has seen embossed upon the blade of an 1805 pattern naval officer's sword:

IN THE RIGHT HAND OF FLETCHER CHRISTIAN I FOUGHT AGAINST TYRANNY ON HMS BOUNTY. 28TH APRIL, 1789

1. *Italian anelace, fifteenth century; excavated in London, 1925.*

2. *Scottish poleaxes and shields, sixteenth century.*

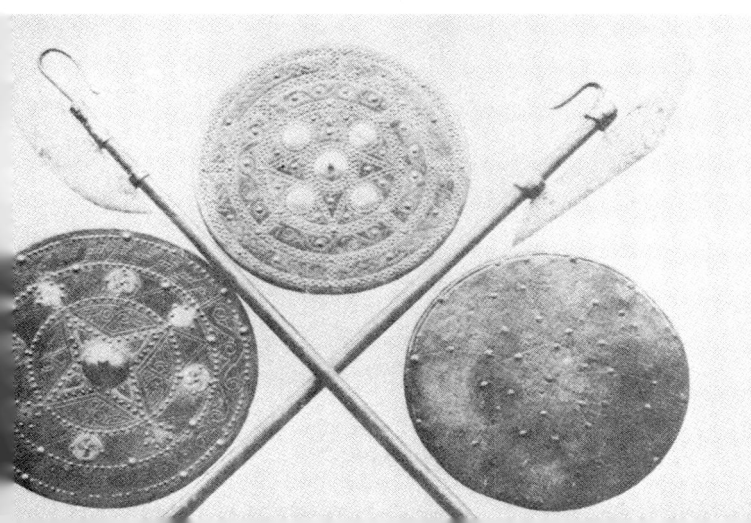

3. *Teutonic sword, thirteenth century.*

4. *Italian sword, fifteenth century.*

5. *Venetian sword, sixteenth century.*

Moroccan sword said to be that of Abou Abd-Allah Mohammed, fifteenth century.

7. *German sword, sixteenth century.*

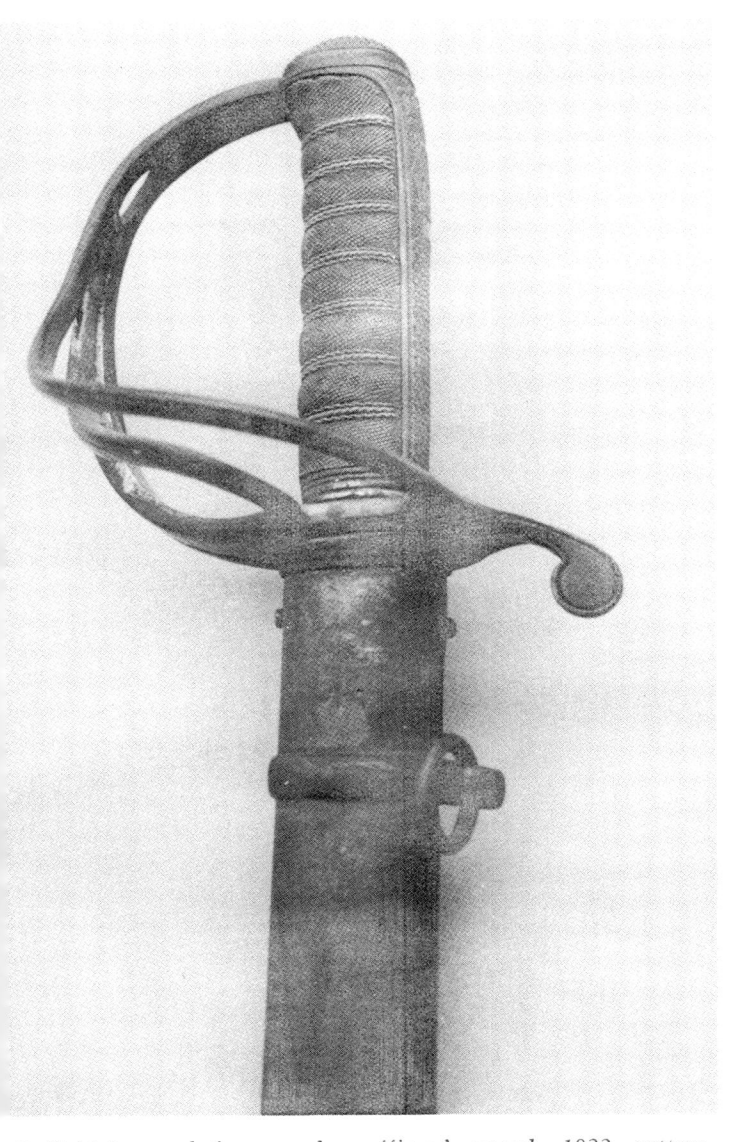

8. *British regulation cavalry officers' sword, 1822 pattern.*

9. English plug bayonets, seventeenth century.

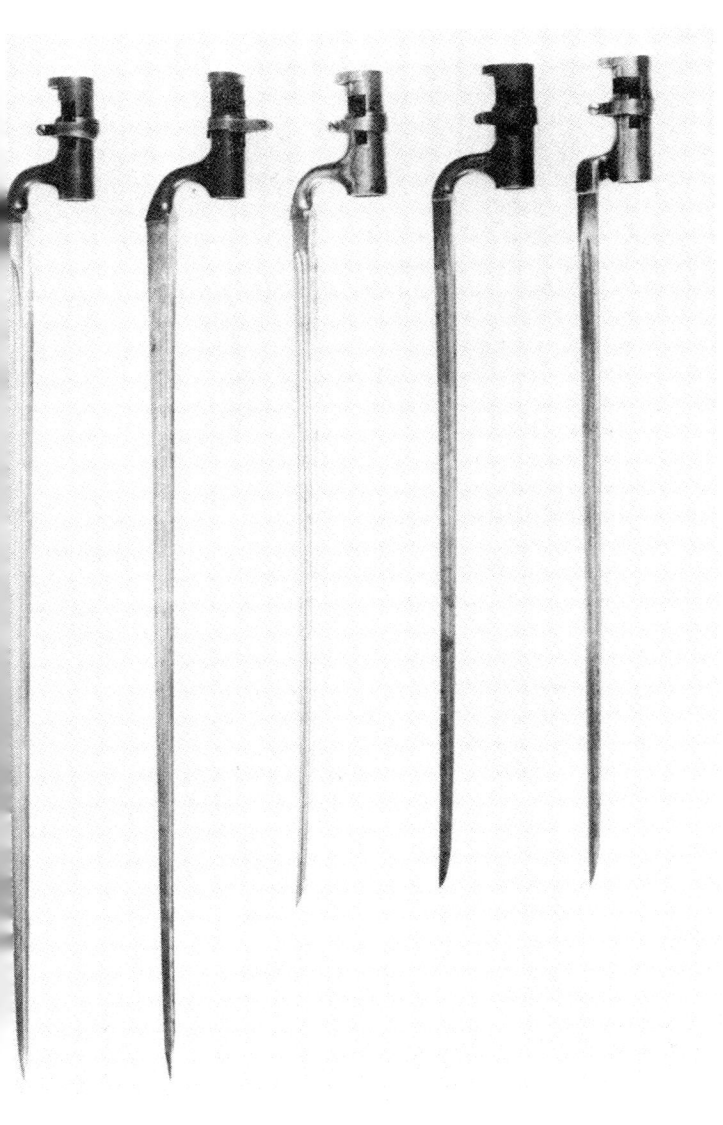

70. British socket bayonets, nineteenth century.

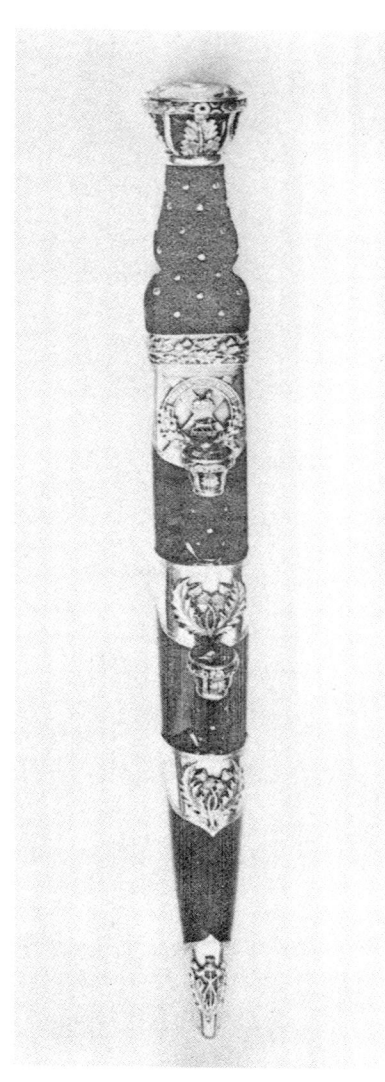

11. Gordon Highlanders officers' dirk, nineteenth century.

12. Regulation court swo[rd] Victorian.

13. *Persian scimitar, nineteenth century.*

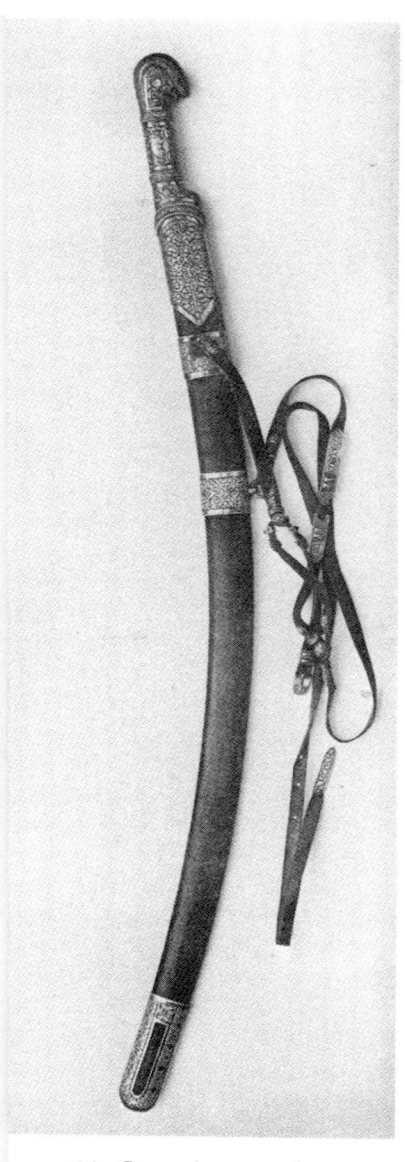

14. Caucasian sword, nineteenth century.

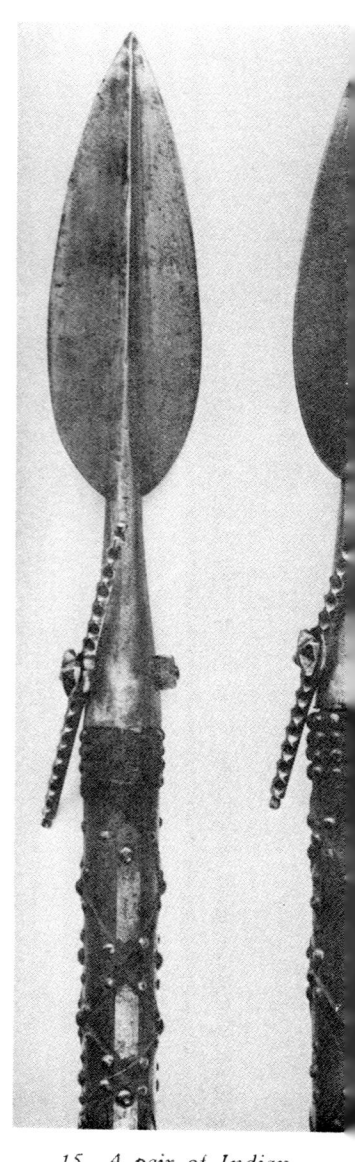

15. A pair of Indian boar-spears with removable crossguards, c. 1860.

16. *Indian double-headed war axe, eighteenth century.*

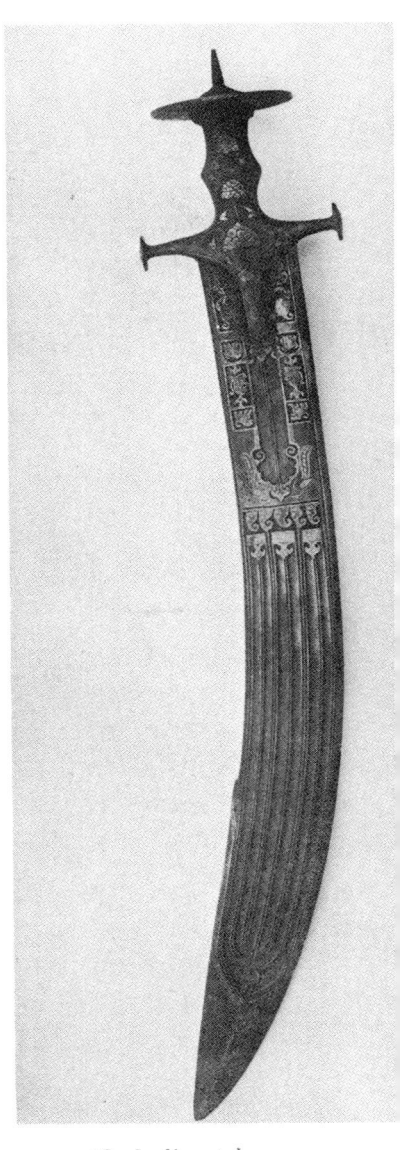

17. *Indian talwar, nineteenth century.*

18. Nepalese kukri with unusual number of additional surgical instruments, nineteenth century.

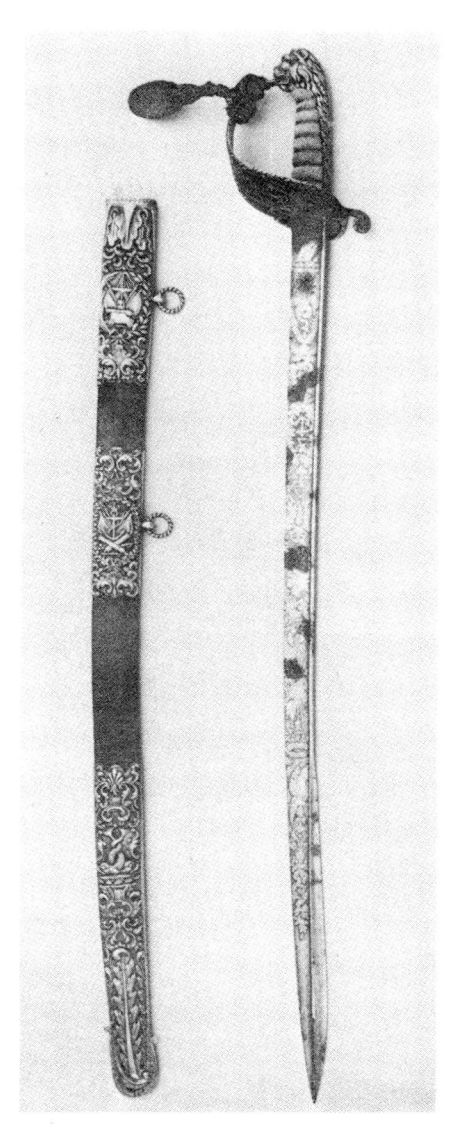

19. *Presentation British naval sword, nineteenth century.*

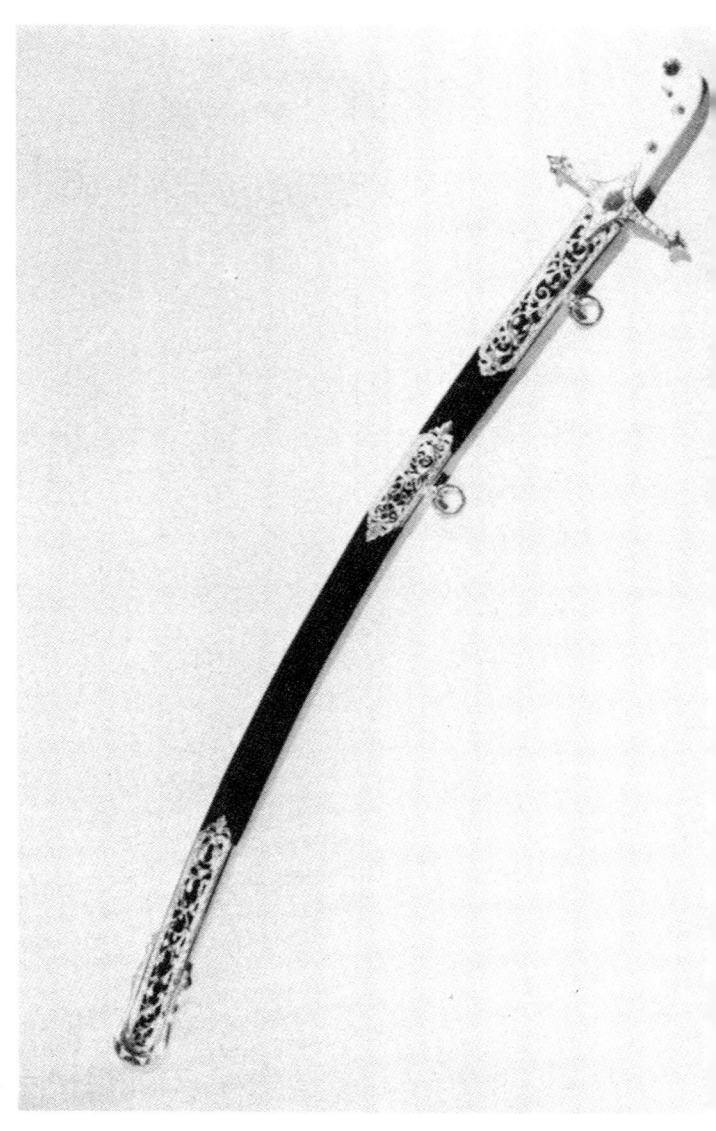

20. Presentation scimitar, British, twentieth century.

6. ORIENTAL AND NATIVE WEAPONS

Other than the edged weapons of the Japanese and a few of the best Indian weapons, examples of oriental manufacture that are to be found in antique shops and salerooms are crude and unsophisticated.

Japan

Japan has one of the oldest continuous civilizations on record and for many hundreds of years it was a feudal society divided into distinct classes. The first and senior class was that of the samurai or warrior, which was hereditary and rather akin to the British peerage. Second in status came the Japanese farmers, then the craftsmen and finally the merchants and shopkeepers.

Although the lower classes were permitted to carry swords and daggers under certain circumstances these were short and known as *wakizashi* and only the samurai were permitted to carry two swords at once and one of these was the *katana* or long sword that was permitted to them alone. The collective name for the pair of swords was a *daisho*. The Japanese dagger, with a handguard or *tsuba*, was known as the *tanto* and although it resembled both the katana and the wakizashi in form it was seldom more than a foot long. The dagger without the tsuba went under the name *aikuchi* and was carried more for utility than for fighting. Should a samurai wish, he could replace the daisho with two other weapons, i.e. a wakizashi and tanto or a wakizashi and *yoroi-toshi* which was a short and thick dagger especially designed to pierce body-armour.

Some of the tanto and aikuchi carried in the sheath the *kodzuka*, a small knife with a highly decorative handle, which was used for skinning and other culinary purposes.

Collecting Japanese swords and reading blades and makers' marks is so complex that it forms a distinct branch of edged weaponry and even the separate parts of swords devoid of blades are much sought after.

India

The vast number of different cultures in India has fostered the design of many edged weapons. The most important group of Indian swords are the *talwars* (plate 17) and they all have the specific type of metal grip and hilt which is small by

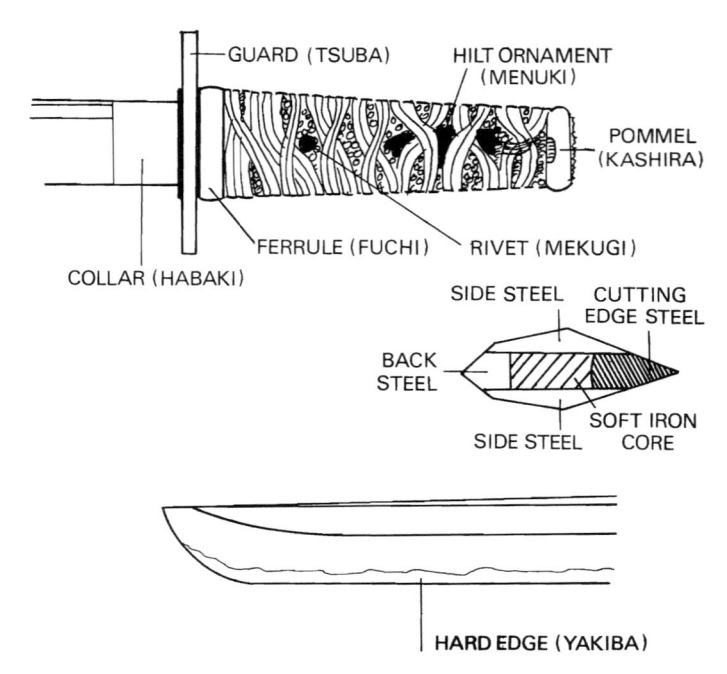

Fig. 10. The parts of the Japanese sword.

European standards and designed for the native hand. Blades for talwars are nearly always curved but there is no set curvature and the breadth of the blades varies from 1 inch to as much as 5 inches measured at the hilt.

Another favourite Indian style was the *shamshir*, from which the mameluke hilt was copied. This scimitar invariably had a narrow curved blade but the curvature of each one was irregular and increased towards the point making it necessary for the scabbard to be slit on the back edge at the mouthpiece in order that the sword might be sheathed.

The traditional close-quarter weapon of the Hindu was the *khouttar*, which had a short broad blade with a strong central rib and was distinguished by its grip which ran at right-angles to the direction of the blade. The Gurkhas of Nepal carried the *kukri* (plate 18) which had a strong incurved blade and varied in length from 14 to as much as 24 inches, the larger ones being used for the religious beheading of cattle. Each kukri had its own custom-made scabbard which contained, as well as the weapon, a skinning knife and a sharpening steel with matching grips.

A weapon that was peculiar to the Sikhs was the *chakram*, which was a quoit with the outer edge sharpened to a razor edge and thrown with deadly accuracy. The *wagnuk* or 'tiger's claw' was a weapon of Indian secret societies and its five parallel blades gave exactly the wounds that would be expected if the victim had been attacked by a wild animal.

In much use on the borders of India during the eighteenth and nineteenth centuries was the war axe (plate 16) and except for the native decoration, often inlaid in gold or silver, many of these look very like the European axes of earlier periods.

Other Asian weapons

The *khinjar* was a dagger that was peculiar to the Caucasians although it originated in Persia. It had a straight double-edged blade some 15 inches long which was comparatively broad for most of its length and carried a central fuller. The grip was usually of bone, ivory or ebony and was in the form of two flat-waisted plates secured by rivets to both sides of the tang.

The *kris* (fig. 11c) was the weapon of Malaya and is distinguished by the wavy and roughly beaten blade and the sharply inclined wooden or ivory handle. The wooden scabbard is especially shaped to accommodate the jagged swell that occurs at the top of the blade.

The *barong* is a weapon that is continually cropping up in sales and is the weapon of the Moros of the Philippines. This has a broad, slightly waved, single-edged blade most crudely made from iron and is fitted into a rough wooden handle that is characterized by having the top end decorated with a bunch of human hair some three inches long.

The Khyber knife comes as might be expected from Afghanistan and is to be found in all lengths from 30 inches down to about 8. The shape is distinctive: it is single-edged with a flat back and tapers evenly from the grip to the acutely sharp point. There is no cross-guard and the grip, which is of two side plates riveted to the tang, slightly resembles a bird's head and is of ivory, camel bone or even jade.

Photographs of Lawrence of Arabia in Arab dress show him carrying a short, sharply curved dagger slung centrally from the belt and lying across the stomach. This is the *jambiya* (fig. 11a), a traditional double-edged razor-sharp dagger suitable for slitting throats. The quality of the weapon can vary from the very rough and ready variety sold cheaply in bazaars to the ornate and bejewelled type with the hilt and mounts in

AFRICAN WEAPONS

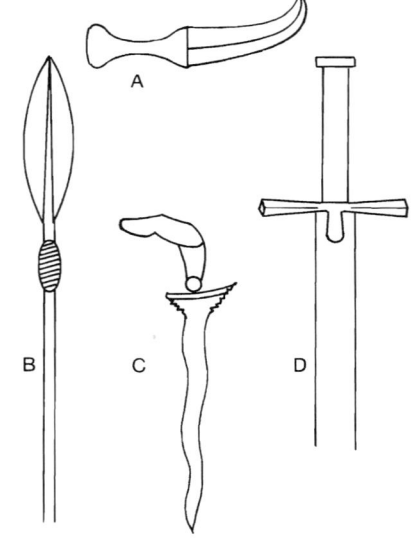

Fig. 11. A. *Arabic jambiya, nineteenth century.* B. *Zulu assegai, nineteenth century.* C. *Malayan kris, nineteenth century.* D. *Sudanese kaskara, nineteenth century.*

gold or silver presented to special guests by Arab potentates.

Africa

The *kaskara* (fig. 11d) was the sword of the Sudanese warriors who fought against the British at the end of the nineteenth century. It is very similar to the crusader's sword of the thirteenth and fourteenth centuries, having a straight, double-edged blade and a simple cross-hilt with the wooden grip bound in leather and the pommel a thick leather disc. These swords, the majority of which were brought home by the victorious armies, may be found with both native and European made blades, the locally made ones usually bearing sun and moon symbols and extracts from the Koran, and the European blades the recognised maker's marks which led to the legend that they were blades that had in fact been abandoned by the original crusaders and had been handed down from father to son as an hereditary possession.

The *assegai* (fig. 11b) was a Zulu spear with a leaf-shaped head, and originally two different types were carried by the warrior. There was a light weapon for throwing and it was not unusual for as many as six of these to be carried by one man. Also there was the short, strong-shafted stabbing assegai, two of which were usually the standard equipment of the fighter. After 1820, when Chaka became king of the Zulus, he reorganised the army and the throwing weapon was abolished. Each man was expected to carry two stabbing spears, a knobkerry and the large hide shield.

America

The Bowie knife (fig. 12) has always been supposed to have been the invention of James Bowie, a legendary American hero. Basically it seems to have been a hunting knife, some 15 inches in blade length with a false edge on the back, but the original weapon is not in existence any longer and any large hunting knife which follows this description is likely to be called by this name.

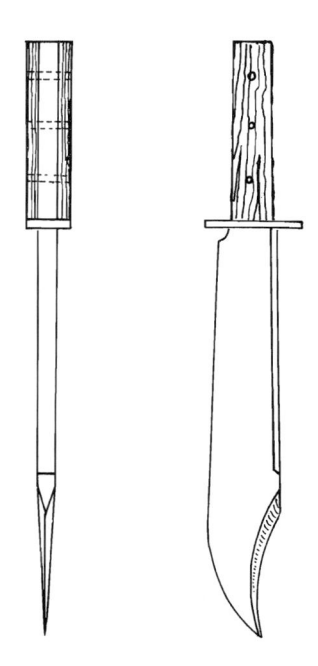

Fig. 12. The Bowie knife.

7. COLLECTING EDGED WEAPONS

Collecting edged weapons generally can be extremely interesting and regardless of the depth of the individual pocket there will seldom be an occasion when it is not possible to add some new and exciting specimen to the collection. However, the subject is so large that it would take a whole museum to house even one example of each and every type of weapon that man has created in the last 4,000 years and it is probably best to start by specialising in either a particular period or a certain type of weapon and as the collection and one's knowledge of the subject grows branch out into adjacent eras or into complementary types of sword, bayonet, knife or pole-arm.

The following list of the various divisions or branches of the subject is neither hardfast nor all-embracing, but the majority of written matter on the subject follows these lines and this will help to limit the number of books the beginner will require and will also narrow the field of his search for specimens to those dealers and auction rooms that specialise in the exotic and rare and those who keep well within their own knowledge and handle the more mundane but nevertheless interesting weapons.

British Military Weapons, 1750, to the present day

This is probably the most satisfying and rewarding subject for the beginner and for those to whom price is a restricting factor although a good maxim is that it is better to purchase one good piece than a roomful of rusty and irreparable junk. There is no dearth of specimens from this period in antique shops and salerooms and the hoarding habits of our Victorian ancestors has assured us of a continuing supply from hitherto neglected attics.

Prices are happily still realistic and the variety of weapons available is large. Swords, lances and bayonets will make up the bulk of the collection which could easily run to 400 or 500 different types and examples. The author's own sword collection which once numbered over 200 was far from complete and there were always variations to be found. The following list of books on the subject may be helpful:
Bayonets, Frederick Stephens, London, 1968.
British Bayonets of World War II, Carter, London, 1969.
British Military Bayonets, Wilkinson-Latham, London, 1967.
British Military Swords, Wilkinson-Latham, London, 1966.

Evolution of Swords, Wilkinson-Latham, London, 1963.
The Lance and Associated Weapons, Parker, London, 1903.
The Naval Officer's Sword, Bosanquet, HMSO (out of print).
Naval Swords, Annis, London, 1970.
Naval Swords and Firearms, May and Kennard, HMSO, 1962.
Regulation Military Swords, Wilkinson-Latham, London, 1970.
Rules and Regulations for Sword Exercise of the Cavalry, reprint, London, 1970.
Sword Collecting for Amateurs, Henderson, London, 1969.
Sword, Lance and Bayonet, Ffoulkes, reprinted London, 1967.

Japanese swords and daggers

This is probably one of the most specialised branches of edged weapon collecting and after the collector has exhausted the supply of World War II military swords that are currently available it can become a satisfying but expensive hobby. The general appeal of Japanese weapons is the almost religious fervour with which they were both manufactured and cared for by the various grades of citizen who were permitted to make or own them and the extremely high level of design and craftsmanship that went into them.

Supplies of first-grade examples of the Japanese swordsmith's art are extremely short and are much sought after by the connoisseurs. Books on the subject are very limited and are not easy to come by and the number of true experts in the field is, as would be expected, quite small. The essential books are:
The Arts of the Japanese Sword, Robinson, London, 1961.
Japanese Sword Blades, Dobree, reprinted London.
Japanese Swordsmiths, Hawley, USA, 1964.
Nippon-To, the Japanese Sword, Hakasui, Tokyo, 1948.
The Primer of Japanese Sword Blades, Robinson, London, 1955.
The Samurai Sword, Yumoto, Tokyo, 1958.
Sword and Samé, Joby and Hogitaro, reprinted London, 1962.

The small sword

The small sword, otherwise known as the town or walking sword, varies in design from plain to ornate and in value from just a few pounds up to many hundreds depending upon the materials used in its manufacture, the name of its maker and, if authenticated, the identity of its owner. The general appeal is to the eye and these little weapons can be things of great beauty and exquisite craftsmanship.

Books on the subject of the small sword are very limited

but there are notable collections in both the Victoria and Albert Museum in London and in the Metropolitan Museum of Art in New York.

Catalogue of European Court and Hunting Swords, Dean, New York, 1929.

A Handbook of Court and Hunting Swords, Carrington-Pierce, London, 1937.

The Small Sword in England, Aylward, reprinted London, 1958.

Asiatic and oriental weapons

The supply of these in both the salerooms and the antique shops never seem to dry up, although the general quality is less than good and the more ornate and better-made weapons are few and far between. Indian weapons seem to predominate due to the long reign of the British in that country and the huge imports that have taken place during the last few years when the Indian government has encouraged the clearing-out of village storehouses. Next come the Sudanese and other African weapons that were brought to England as souvenirs after the nineteenth century wars in that continent and then possibly the swords and daggers of the Malayan archipelago.

Very little authoritative written matter exists on this subject and the correct cataloguing of specimens is difficult, even for museum curators.

An Illustrated Handbook of Indian Arms, Egerton, London, 1880.

Indian and Oriental Armour, Egerton, reprinted London, 1968.

The Indian Sword, Rawson, Copenhagen, 1967.

Kris and other Malay Weapons, Gardner, Singapore, 1936.

Early stone, bronze and iron weapons

This is an extremely limited field for the collector although flint arrowheads continue to be found throughout the world and, one would guess, are still being manufactured for sale to the unsuspecting. The remainder of these weapons are on the list of rarities and when occasionally genuine pieces appear in the salerooms they fetch prices that are very high.

The subject has received much attention from authors in the past but this means that the majority of books are long out of print and may not even appear in county lending libraries.

Arms and Armour of the Greeks, Snodgrass, London, 1967.

European Arms and Armour, Volume I, Laking, London, 1920.

The Roman Soldier, Catchpole, privately printed, London, 1948.
Weapons of War, Demmin, London, 1870.

Medieval European weapons

This is an extremely well documented branch of weapon collecting and many expert authors continue to contribute to the subject. Examples of the swords, axes, pole-arms and daggers of the period exist in very many public collections and in particular the Tower of London and the Metropolitan Museum of Art in New York display some of the finest pieces that were made. Genuine weapons have always fetched high prices at auction and these continue to rise as the demand increases. Victorian armourers were adept at making very good copies to fill the demand for wall decoration in the large country houses of the period and these copies are now in fairly good supply but the serious collector would hesitate to add them to a collection of genuine pieces.

The Archaeology of Weapons, Oakeshott, London, 1964.
Arms and Armament, Ffoulkes, Oxford, 1948.
The Book of the Sword, Burton, London, 1884.
British and Foreign Arms and Armour, Ashdown, London, 1909.
Edged Weapons, Wilkinson, London, 1970.
European Arms and Armour, Volumes II-V, Laking, London, 1920.
The Sword and the Centuries, Hutton, London, 1901.
The Sword in the Age of Chivalry, Oakeshott, London, 1964.

Weapons of Nazi Germany

This is a subject that does not have universal appeal but the collectors of these pieces are amongst the keenest and most ardent of all military collectors. The enormous production of swords and daggers that were manufactured in Solingen to bolster up the pageantry of the Third Reich have now been dispersed throughout the world, the majority as souvenirs, and therefore prices for genuine pieces are high.

A word of warning to would-be collectors. Some of the original patterns and tools are still in existence in Solingen and there is a thriving trade in the production of replicas, some of which inevitably find their way into the salerooms and antique dealers' shops. Amongst the books that are available are the following:

The Daggers and Edged Weapons of Hitler's Germany, Atwood, Berlin, 1965.
Swords of Hitler's Third Reich, Angola, London, 1969.

IDENTIFYING WEAPONS

GENERAL READING

European and American Arms, Blair, London, 1962.
Inventory of the Tower of London Armouries, Ffoulkes, London, 1916.
Swords and Daggers, Wilkinson, London, 1967.
Warriors' Weapons, Buehn, New York, 1962.

8. THE IDENTIFICATION OF EDGED WEAPONS

Probably the most difficult task for the collector is the correct identification and cataloguing of the various pieces of the collection and yet this can be the most pleasing part of the hobby.

Many times the author has been asked to identify a sword from photographs and a mass of letters, symbols and marks that appear on various parts of the weapon and as no one can keep such knowledge in his head it is only after patient search through books that the answer emerges.

The earliest of weapons seldom bear any sort of marks that will positively identify their country of origin or their makers and it is only by reference to the type and shape of recorded examples that the owner will be able to frame the entry in his own chronicles. Once, however, we get to the medieval period we find that the armourers nearly always marked their work with their names or insignia and in the countries where the armourer's was a highly respected trade, such as Germany, Italy, Spain or France, the mark of the guild of armourers is much used.

Fig. 13. Some typical examples of marks on weapons: A. *Japanese swordmaker's mark.* B. *Guild mark of the Augsburg armourers.* C. *Running wolf mark of Passau.* D. *Italian armourer's scorpion mark, sixteenth century.* E. *Mark of Juan Martinez, of Toledo, Spain.* F. *German mark on a sixteenth century crossbow.* G. *Mark on a sixteenth century war hammer.* H. *Mark on the sword of Chevalier de St. Georges, proclaimed King James III of England at Scone, 1715.* I. *Wolf mark on a sixteenth century sword made by Bregio.* J. *Mark on the blade of a rapier by Caino, sixteenth*

MAKERS MARKS

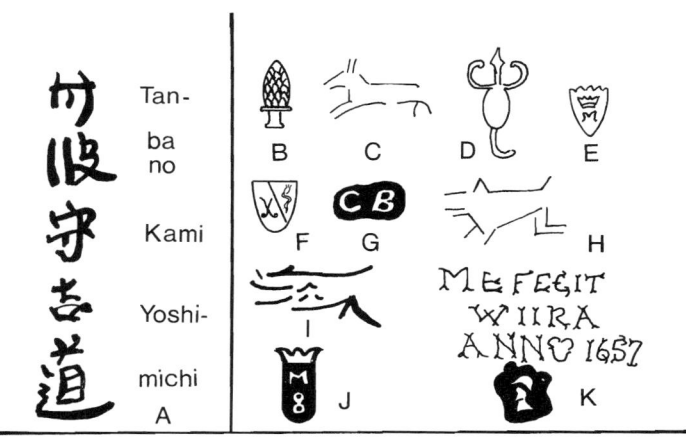

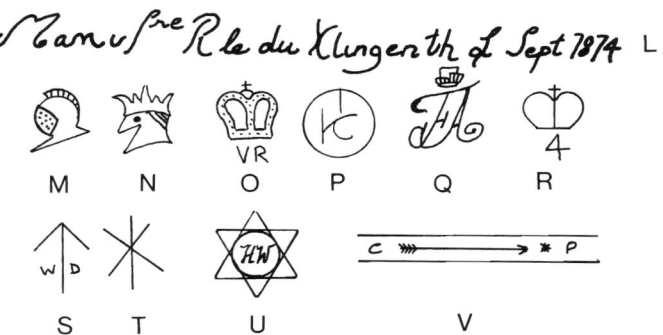

century. K. *Mark on a seventeenth century executioner's sword.* L. *French mark for the arsenal at Klingenthal.* M. *and* N. *Nineteenth century marks of Weyersberg of Solingen.* O. *Victorian reign mark.* P. *French Klingenthal mark, 1800.* Q. *Cipher of Frederick of Prussia, 1800.* R. *British armament inspector's mark and number, nineteenth and twentieth centuries.* S. *British War Department mark.* T. *British obsolete weapon mark.* U. *Proof mark of Henry Wilkinson.* V. *Centre of percussion mark for blades.*

MAKERS MARKS

The era of the regulation weapon should be much easier for the collector but regrettably it is not always as simple as that. Designs of weapon amongst European countries often followed from those of other nations which were successful in battle. Furthermore many countries purchased their weapons from the great arsenals such as Solingen in Germany and St. Etienne in France which, in order to achieve economic prices, sold the same style of weapon to many countries.

British, French and German weapons are usually the easiest to identify because of the use of regimental insignia on the British, the place and date of manufacture on the French and the use of the Kaiser's cipher on the German. American weapons are inclined to follow the German in style, as are South American, which were made exclusively in Solingen for many years and, except for inscriptions on the blades, are identical to many that were carried by the Prussian armies of the late nineteenth century.

Japanese weapons are of course of such a style that their country of origin is easily identified and it is only after the bamboo peg is carefully removed from the grip and it is slid from the tang of the blade that the true task of identity is revealed. All first-class Japanese swords and daggers bear the full story of their manufacture carefully chiselled into the tang in Japanese characters and it is the reading of blades that is one of the most fascinating parts of this hobby. The majority of Japanese sword blades that will be found in Europe date from the Shinto or 'new sword' period that lasted from 1537 to 1867, and on all these the name of the smith, the place of manufacture and the date are inscribed. In some cases there is also added such information as 'tested on the bodies of three malefactors'.

Figure 13 shows some of the marks that have been found on weapons and gives the collector some idea of the type of identification marks that he will have to decipher. The inventories of the Tower of London armouries mentioned in chapter 7 and *Weapons of War* by Demmin also illustrate many of these armourers' marks.

The following are marks that may be found on issue British military weapons but the list is so large that it is only possible to give the styles of marking here. The letter sizes that were used on edged weapons were laid down by regulation as 5/64 inch high and there were two sets of markings (sometimes more if the weapons had been withdrawn from one regiment and then re-issued to another). Ordnance marks gave the number of the month and the last two figures of the year of issue, e.g. '5/82' would be May, 1882, and the Corps mark gave either the numbers or letter cipher of the regiment or both, e.g. 'C.17L' which would be C Squadron 17th Lancers.

Swords were invariably marked on the tail of the guard at the back of the hilt and on the top of the scabbard if metal, or on the mouthpiece if leather. Bayonets were identified by marking on the pommel, or on the top tube if socket type, and on the mouthpiece of the scabbard, and lances had their marks on the shoe.

Prior to 1881 the infantry regiments of the British army were known by numbers but after that date these were dropped in favour of letters. This means that a sword or bayonet prior to 1881 would be identifiable as belonging to the Devonshire Regiment if it were marked '11' and after that date if marked 'Dvn.' Similarly a Middlesex Regiment bayonet would be '57' before 1881, and simply 'Mx' after that date.

Yeomanry and territorial units had more letters than regulars and these were divided by a line thus $\frac{Y}{SK.H}$ which is the mark of the Suffolk Hussars, or $\frac{R.A.M.C.}{1ST. M.G.H.}$ which is the 1st Manchester General Hospital, Royal Army Medical Corps, Territorial Army.

In addition to the unit marks others may be found that identify the maker, examples being GILL, DAWES, MOLE and WILKINSON, and these are usually on the shoulder of the blade. On the tang of the blade and on the underneath of the guard near the tang hole may be found the initials of the actual smith or hilt maker who made that part of the weapon and these are usually two letters only such as TB, Wilkinson's famous bladesmith Tom Beasley.

The practice of individual craftsmen using marks came into being in England and Germany when sword cutlers ordered the various parts of weapons from outworkers, assembled them together in their own workshops and marked them with their own names thus taking the credit for the work which had been done mainly by others.

INDEX

Figures in italic denote illustrations

Afghanistan 51
Africa 52-53, 56
Aikuchi 49
America 23, 24, 26, 53, 60
Anelace 16, *pl. 1*
Angon 10
Arab weapons 51-52
Arrowheads 3, 4, *5*, 7, 56
Assegai 52
Assyria 5
Axe 3, 4, *5*, 10, 11, 23, 30, 51, 57, *pl. 16*
Backsword 20, 21
Baker rifle 29
Barong 51
Baselard 18
Basket hilt 18, 19, 21, 25, 26
Bastard sword 18,19
Battleaxe 3, 4, *5*, 10, 11, 12
Bayonet 13, 24, 26, 27, 29-30, 54, 55, 61, *pl. 9-10*
Belgium 9
Bill 14
Billhook 30
Boer War 29
Bohemia 20
Books on edged weapons 54-58
Bow and arrow 10, 23
Bowie knife 53
Braquemart 20
Broad-axe 11
Broadsword 18, 19, 21, 26
Bronze Age 4-7, 13, 14, 56
Brown Bess 29
Brunswick rifle 29
Calendar sword 22
Caucasian weapons 51, *pl. 14*
Celts 3, 4, 5
Chakram 51
Cinquedea 16, 20
Claymore 18, 21
Colichemerde 22
Commandos 30
Corsèque 14
Corsica 14
Court sword 22, 56, *pl. 12*

Crimean War 27, 32
Crossbow 23
Cross-guard 8, 10, 11, 12, 13, 14, 18, 20, 28, 51
Crusaders 30, 52
Cup-hilt 19, 20
Dagger 3, 4, *5*, 6, 8, 12, *17*, 18, 23, 29, 32, 51, 55, 56, 57, 58, 60
Daisho 49
Danes 4, 10-12
Dart 9
Dirk 19, *pl.11*
Duels 19
Dusack 20
East India Company 31
Egypt 4, 5, 6, 7
Estoc 20
Fabergé 22
Fairburn and Sykes knife 30
Falchion 15, *17*, 19, 25
Fauchard 13
Flamberge 18
Flints 3, 4, *5*, 6, 7, 56
Framea 10
France 9, 14, 24, 28, 60
Francisca 10
Franks 9-10
Germany 9, 14, 18, 26, 57, 60, 61, *pl. 7*
Gisarme 13, 14
Glaive 14, *15*
Great-sword 18
Greeks 7-8, *9*, 56
Guards, Brigade of 27
Gurkhas 50
Halberd 13, *15*
Hand-and-a-half sword 18
Hanger 25
Hatchet 3, 4, 5, 23
Hilts 6, 16, 20, 22, 24, 25, 26, 32, 51, 61
Holland 9
Horse Guards 28
Household Cavalry 29
Hungary 25

India 26, 27, 28, 31, 49-51, 56, pl. 15-17
Ireland 27
Iron Age 5
Italy 9, 14, 19, 20, 21, 60, pl. 1, pl. 4
Jambiya 51, 52
Japan, 49, 50, 55, 59, 60
Javelin 5, 7, 8, 10
Kaskara 52
Katana 49
Kelto-Gallic weapons 4, 7
Khinjar 51
Khouttar 50
Khyber knife 51
Knives 3, 4, 30, 31, 53, 54
Kodzuka 49
Kris 51, 52, 56
Kukri 50, pl. 18
Lance 3, 5, 7, 8, 10, 12, 14, 18, 27, 28, 29, 54, 55
Linstock 23
Mace 12
Main- gauche 18, 19
Malaya 51, 56
Malchus 20
Mameluke sword 28, 32, 50
Marks on weapons 59, 58-61
Martini-Henry rifle 29
Middle Ages 13-19, 57
Minié Enfield rifle 29
Miséricorde 18
Mohammed 20
Moros 51
Mortuary sword 22
Mussulmans 20
Nazi weapons 57
Neolithic period 3, 4
Nepal 50, pl. 18
Normans 12, 14
Palaeolithic period 3
Palestine 29
Panzerbrecher 18
Parazonium 8
Partisan 13, 16
Patriotic Fund 31
Persia 5, 51, pl. 13
Philippines 51

Pike 3, 13-14, 29
Pillow sword 22
Pilum 8, 10
Plug bayonet 29, pl. 9
Poland 25, 28
Pole-arms 19, 23, 24, 54, 57
Poleaxe 13, 15, pl. 2
Pommels 6, 8, 10, 11, 14, 15, 17, 18, 20, 22, 25, 26, 61
Presentation swords 30-32
Prussia 24-60
Quillons 11, 16, 18, 20, 25
Ranseur 14
Rapier 19-20, 22
Regulation weapons 24-30, pl. 8
Rifle regiments 27
Romans 8-9, 57
Royal Small Arms Factory 24
Sabre 20, 26
St. Etienne 60
Samurai 49
Saxons 10-12
Scabbard 6, 7, 8, 9, 10, 12, 24, 28, 32, 50, 51, 61
Scandinavia 7
Schiavona 21
Scimitar 16-17, 19, 32, 50, pl. 31, pl. 20
Scotland 18, 19, 21, 23, 26, pl. 2
Scythe 14, 15
Shamshir 50
Sikhs 51
Small-sword 21-22, 55
Snider rifle 29
Socket bayonet 29, 61, pl. 10
Solingen 31, 57, 59, 60
Spain 19, 20, 60
Spatha 8
Spear 6, 8, 10, pl. 15
Spearhead 4, 6, 7, 8
Spontoon 23
Staff weapons 23
Stalingrad 30
Stiletto 18
Stirrup hilt 26
Stone Age 3-4, 6, 56

Sudan 52, 56
Swiss 14, 17
Sword-breaker 19
Syrians 7
Talwar 51, *pl. 17*
Tanto 49
Taper-axe 11
Toledo 20, *59*
Tomahawk 23
Tower of London 24, 57, 60
Town sword 22, 25
Trafalgar swords 31
Trench weapons 30
Tsuba 49
Turks 25

Two-handed sword 17-18
Venice 21, *pl. 5*
Voulge 14, *15*
Wagnuk 51
Wakizashi 49
Walking-sword 22, 25
War-scythe 14, *15*
Wilkinson Sword Company 30, 61
Woolwich 29
Yeomen of the Guard 13
Yoroi-toshi 49
Zulus 52, 53
Zweihander 17-18, 19